In memory of Maurice Smith (1903–2005),
and for his granddaughter Jennifer.—R.M.

To the memory of Winfield Hatch and William Harvey Hatch,
who kept our small farm in the family as long as they could.—M.A.

G. P. PUTNAM'S SONS
A division of Penguin Young Readers Group.
Published by The Penguin Group.
Penguin Group (USA) Inc., 375 Hudson Street, New York, NY 10014, U.S.A.
Penguin Group (Canada), 90 Eglinton Avenue East, Suite 700, Toronto, Ontario, Canada M4P 2Y3
(a division of Pearson Penguin Canada Inc.).
Penguin Books Ltd, 80 Strand, London WC2R 0RL, England.
Penguin Ireland, 25 St. Stephen's Green, Dublin 2, Ireland (a division of Penguin Books Ltd.).
Penguin Group (Australia), 250 Camberwell Road, Camberwell, Victoria 3124, Australia
(a division of Pearson Australia Group Pty Ltd).
Penguin Books India Pvt Ltd, 11 Community Centre, Panchsheel Park, New Delhi - 110 017, India.
Penguin Group (NZ), 67 Apollo Drive, Mairangi Bay, Auckland 1311, New Zealand
(a division of Pearson New Zealand Ltd.)
Penguin Books (South Africa) (Pty) Ltd, 24 Sturdee Avenue, Rosebank, Johannesburg 2196, South Africa.
Penguin Books Ltd, Registered Offices: 80 Strand, London WC2R 0RL, England.

Library of Congress Cataloging-in-Publication Data
Michelson, Richard.
Tuttle's Red Barn : the story of America's oldest family farm / by Richard Michelson ; illustrated by Mary Azarian.   p. cm.
1. Tuttle family—Juvenile literature. 2. Family farms—New Hampshire—Dover—Juvenile literature. 3. Dover (N.H.)—
History—Juvenile literature. 4. Tuttle's Red Barn (Farm)—Juvenile literature. I. Azarian, Mary. II. Title.
F44.D7M53 2007   975.1'4—dc22   2007007514

ISBN 978-0-399-24354-7
1 3 5 7 9 10 8 6 4 2
First Impression

TUTTLE'S RED BARN

The Story of America's Oldest Family Farm

In exchange for farming the
Land and paying his taxes
I hereby give young
John Tuttle
a quarter acre house lot
plus seven additional acres
for planting in
Dover New Hampshire
His Majesty
King Charles I

by RICHARD MICHELSON   illustrated by MARY AZARIAN

G. P. PUTNAM'S SONS

John Tuttle *1ˢᵗ Generation (1616–1683)*

JOHN TUTTLE loved adventure, and he didn't mind hard work. "There's a *new* England across the ocean," he told his parents, "where land is plentiful and free."

After two long months at sea, the weather worsened and the ship anchored off the coast of Maine. Now John watched from shore as the storm battered the hull against the rocks. In his hands, he held all that remained of his possessions: his father's ax and the two pewter candleholders his mother had given him after they'd hugged good-bye.

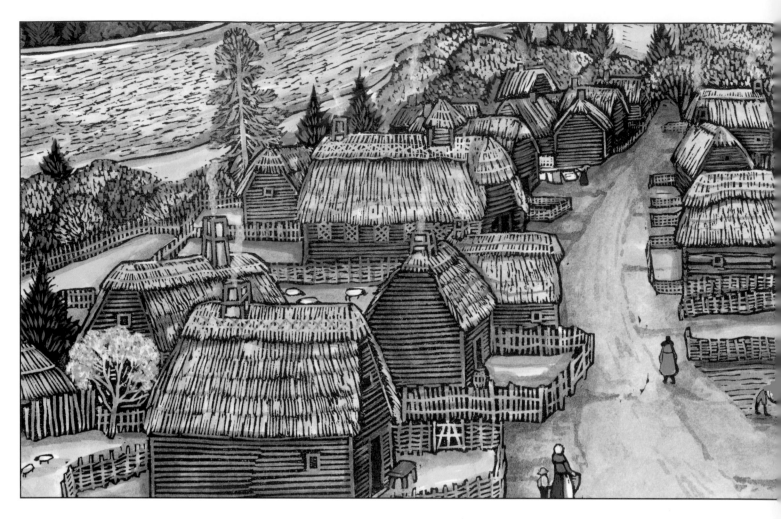

John walked for ten days, until he found twenty cabins clustered between two rivers. This was Dover, the largest settlement in New Hampshire.

With his neighbors' help, John cleared and plowed his land and built a small cabin. The thatched roof would keep the house warm in winter and cool in summer. John thought it was the perfect place to raise a family.

On the Sabbath, John would dress in his new high tapered hat and fasten his breeches below his knees. One Sunday, on his way to the meetinghouse, he passed his neighbor's daughter, Dorothy. John daydreamed about her throughout the whole three-hour sermon, and afterward, he walked her home.

John and Dorothy fell in love, and married. They had four children and named their youngest boy John Jr.

JOHN JR. didn't mind hard work. By the time he was eight, he was already preparing the cabin for the long winter. He filled the chinks in the logs with rock and clay, while his sisters rubbed linseed oil on the paper windows to let in the light and keep out the rain.

Now John Jr. was getting hungry. He loved the smell of his mother's rabbit stew. She was proud of the new brick hearth, with cranes to swing the kettles on and off the fire safely.

In the spring, John Jr. helped his father clear two extra acres. They already owned twenty. They fertilized the soil with oysters and grew all their own peas, potatoes, pears, pumpkins and parsnips. They traded their extra pumpkins to the Penacook Indians for beaver skins to send back to England.

John Jr. grew up and took over the family farm. His father had explained that the youngest son had the best hope of living the longest and keeping the land in the Tuttle family. John Jr. married and had eight children.

James Tuttle *3rd Generation (1683–1709)*

Ten Tuttles now shared the small one-room cabin. It was getting crowded. **JAMES** couldn't wait for his older brothers to marry and move downriver to build their own cabins. This would help the settlement of Dover continue to grow, even though the Indians said the settlers were clearing too much of the forest.

One day James saw a fire in the distance. The town mill was burning, and half a dozen of his neighbors' cabins were also in flames. Then, *Pow! Pow! Pow!* James heard gunshots. He joined his father and brothers as they chased the attackers away from the Tuttle farm. "The Penacooks killed twenty-three people," his brother Thomas shouted. "And they took twenty-nine prisoners." That meant more than one quarter of the townspeople were dead or missing. James was glad his family was safe.

James grew up and he took over the family farm. He married his childhood sweetheart, Rose. They named their daughter Phoebe and their son Elijah.

Elijah Tuttle   *4ᵗʰ Generation (1708–1787)*

ELIJAH was used to hard work. His father, James, had died when Elijah was a baby, and even though the neighbors helped when they could, there were never enough hands to work around the farm. Today, Elijah shingled the sagging roof. It seemed like the house was falling down faster than he could fix it. He plowed the fields, walking behind the tired old ox. He planted squash and rhubarb and beets and beans. He traded barrels of pumpkins and two pigs to the Pinkhams in exchange for a cow. Then he carved the Tuttle "T" on the new cattle's horns.

In the spring Elijah tapped the maples. He boiled the sap and delivered syrup to the Varneys. Their daughter Esther was in the kitchen, carding wool.

By summertime, Esther and Elijah were in love. They married and had four sons: James, Benjamin, Samuel and William. Finally, Elijah would have plenty of help around the farm.

William Tuttle *5th Generation (1750–1834)*

It was already a lucky day. **WILLIAM** had found three arrowheads buried by the pond. "I bet Indians lived right here once," he told his father, Elijah, as they hoisted up barrels of parsnips, pears and potatoes they had picked to help feed the troops.

William wished he could ride the wagon into Boston, but he was needed around the farm. He missed his older brothers. They'd gone off to fight for the colonies in June of 1774, but they told William they hoped to be back before the harvest.

By the time his brothers returned, America had declared its
independence. William was proud that his father, with 150 acres, was
one of the largest landowners in New Hampshire. Except for the salt and
pepper, there was nothing on the dinner table that they had not grown or
raised on their own land.

It was fun to have the family together again. But the cabin was crowded, so William and his brothers decided to build a bigger farmhouse. They felled the trees and carted most of the timber upriver to the new sawmill. They bartered butter and cheese with the blacksmith for door hinges and fireplace tools. They built four large bedrooms, a porch, and a rocking chair for their father, Elijah. William thought this house would be the perfect place to raise a family after his brothers married and moved downriver.

Today, William was excited. He knew that nine of the thirteen colonies needed to ratify the new country's Constitution for it to become law. And he was proud that on June 21, 1788, New Hampshire was the ninth to vote yes. Now it seemed like all two thousand Dover citizens had gathered on Huckleberry Hill to celebrate. Nine cannon salutes were fired nine minutes apart, followed by nine hip-hip-hoorays. William was finally a citizen of the United States. So were his wife, Anna, their three daughters, and their young sons, Ira and Joseph.

Joseph Tuttle *6ᵗʰ Generation (1786–1874)*

As **JOSEPH** grew up, he couldn't remember a time that he wasn't an American. Now, on the last day of the century, Joseph jumped out of bed. It was 6:30 in the morning, and his sisters were already in the kitchen, planning the party. Phoebe was churning butter, while Rose dipped wax for the candles and Sarah polished the pewter ware. She handed Joseph two candleholders to set on the mantle. "Careful," she told him. "Our great-great-great-grandfather carried those here from England over 150 years ago."

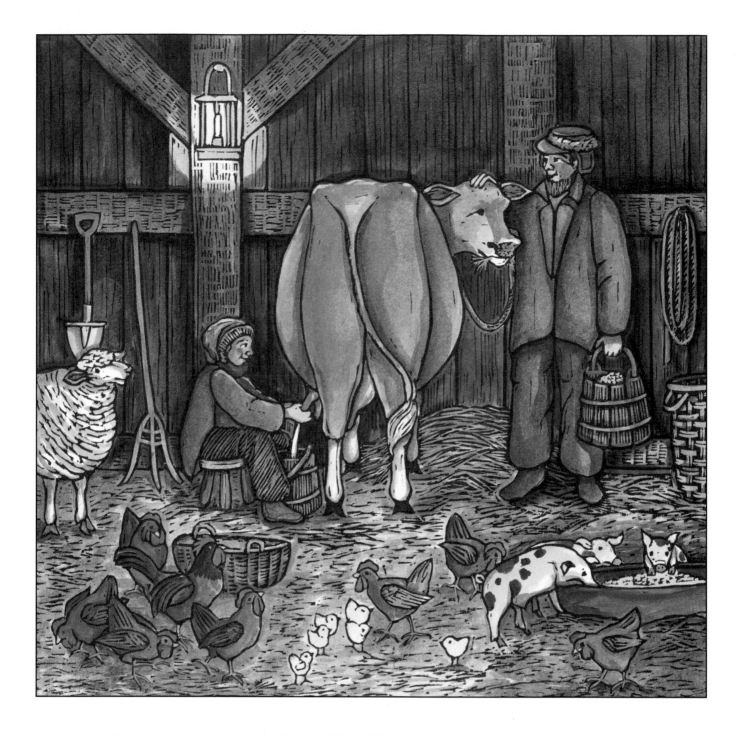

Joseph ran over to the barn. He milked Bessie while his father fed the new baby pigs. "It's getting crowded in here," Joseph said. His father, William, laughed. "This barn used to be my home," he said. "It was big enough for me, Grandpa, Grandma and all three of your uncles." He petted the old milk cow. "My bed was right here."

Joseph grew up and he took over the family farm. He married his neighbor, Sarah Pinkham. They had five children, Eliza, Asa Chase, Steven, William Penn, and the youngest, Joseph Edward.

Joseph Edward Tuttle *7ᵗʰ Generation (1835–1874)*

JOSEPH EDWARD hated getting up in the morning, but even on the coldest days, there was work to be done to prepare for winter. He picked up his father's ax and began to split and stack the firewood. Joseph Edward wished the runaway slaves could help with the chores, but they had to stay hidden all day.

Now it was dark again and he and his brothers stood guard as their father, Joseph, unlocked the trapdoor under the bedroom closet. Joseph Edward lit his lantern. He and his father led the men off Tuttle land. In the woods north of Dover they heard the secret whistle. "Good luck," Joseph Edward said. He hoped these slaves would make it all the way to freedom.

The years passed, and Joseph Edward wished that he, too, could head off on a new adventure. Since the railroad came, some of his neighbors had left Dover and headed west, where land was plentiful and free. Others moved to Worcester for a job in the mills. "I only have to work twelve hours a day," one friend wrote, "and I get Sundays off every week!" Joseph Edward couldn't imagine having that much free time; a whole day to daydream and invent things.

Today, though, Joseph Edward wasn't working on the farm. It was the second day of March, 1860, and Mr. Abraham Lincoln was arriving in Dover! Joseph Edward set up his cart at the depot. He filled it with jugs of maple syrup to sell to the crowd.

No one paid him any mind until Mr. Lincoln stepped out of the caboose
to buy some famous New Hampshire "sweet water."

Joseph Edward married and had two sons. He named them Lewis
Edward and George William.

George William Tuttle 8th Generation (1865–1937)

GEORGE WILLIAM loved all of his uncle William Penn's moneymaking and laborsaving ideas, even though they never managed to make any extra money, and work on the farm was as hard as ever. After his father Joseph Edward's death, George William helped his uncle gather cranberries from the bog, and grapes from their vineyard. It was fun to run the first cider mill in Dover, right here on their land.

George William was also proud that they had built the town's only
greenhouse. Who cared that most of his neighbors preferred to barter and
no one wanted to buy Tuttle flowers, cranberries, grapes or cider?

When George William grew up, he took over the family farm. He and
his wife, Jane, had five children. They named one son William Penn after
George William's uncle.

William Penn Tuttle *9th Generation (1891–1978)*

PENN loved to wake up early and he didn't mind hard work. Today he helped his father fill their barrels with apples, potatoes and cabbage. Then Penn lifted up the jugs of cider and the bottles of maple syrup while his father hitched Old Sally to the wagon.

They rode into town and sold everything they'd brought to Gil Caswell, who ran the grocery. "I wish I could pay you more," Gil said. Penn held out his hand and took the money. It barely covered the cost of the seeds. The giant farms out west, with their big new machines, could reap huge harvests, so most of the neighboring farms had shut down. Now it was cheaper to buy food than to grow your own.

One morning, as he walked toward the barn, Penn couldn't
believe his eyes. Parked outside was the first Model T truck he had
ever seen.

"We'll match anyone on quantity and beat them on quality," his father said. Penn turned the crank until the motor started. Then he climbed in and honked the horn.

Hugh Tuttle *10ᵗʰ Generation (1921–2002)*

Behind the rusty old Ford, Penn's teenage son, **HUGH**, was splitting wood for the long New England winter. He stacked it in the empty old barn that used to house the cattle.

Hugh knew his father expected him to take over the farm someday, but Hugh wanted to see the world. He couldn't wait until September, when he'd be heading off to Harvard.

Hugh studied hard, but he missed the rural way of life. He couldn't wait to return to the family farm. When he got home, he joked, "I wasn't homesick, I was farmsick."

Hugh got married and had three children. He bought a tractor to help plow more land, and he added four irrigation ponds so the crops wouldn't have to wait for the rain. As the years passed, he saw more and more city dwellers driving through the hills of New Hampshire. Some were the children and grandchildren of the old farmers. They were looking for what their families had left behind.

"Maybe they'd like to stop for a glass of cider," Hugh told his son, Will, and his daughters, Lucy and Rebecca. "Or bring some of our cranberries or fresh flowers back home."

"The road goes by the old empty barn," Hugh's wife, Joan, said. "We can paint it red and put up a big sign—HOME GROWN." She was standing near the same spot where, over 300 years ago, John Tuttle had built his cabin.

WILL placed the squash next to the pumpkins and the beans. "Look, Lucy, a New York license plate." The car stopped and a couple got out. "I used to visit my granddaddy up this way," the man told his wife. "I sure miss the beautiful countryside and fresh air." He picked up two pounds of berries. "Food sure tastes better when it's home grown." Another car pulled up. And a third.

Will grew up and he took over the family farm. Every year more and more visitors stopped by. They'd all heard about the Tuttles' fresh vegetables and fruits.

Will and Lucy added a nursery onto the Red Barn, and a store stocked with things like hand-spun wool, hand-dipped wax candles, hand-churned butter and genuine maple syrup.

Grayson Tuttle *12th Generation (1997–)*

Will's son **GRAYSON** woke at 3:30, like most farmers.
He pulled on his boots and headed out to the fields. Soon, the field crew would arrive, but they could never grow as much on the 240-acre Tuttle Farm as they needed, so Grayson climbed into the truck and sat next to his father. They drove an hour to the farmers' market, where they picked out only the freshest fruits and vegetables to sell at the Red Barn.

By 6:00 A.M., when they got back home, the parking lot was already half full.

Grayson's aunt Lucy was inside stocking the shelves. She placed the cheese she'd imported from Europe next to the fine wine and exotic plants.

Someone asked Grayson about the pewter candleholders. "These are just like the ones we have on our mantle at home," he told her. "My great-great-great-great-great-great-great-great-great-grandfather brought them over from England."

"Then you must be Will's boy," she said. "I hope you're planning to take over the farm someday."

Grayson didn't mind hard work, and he thought this was the perfect place to raise a family. "I sure hope so," he said.

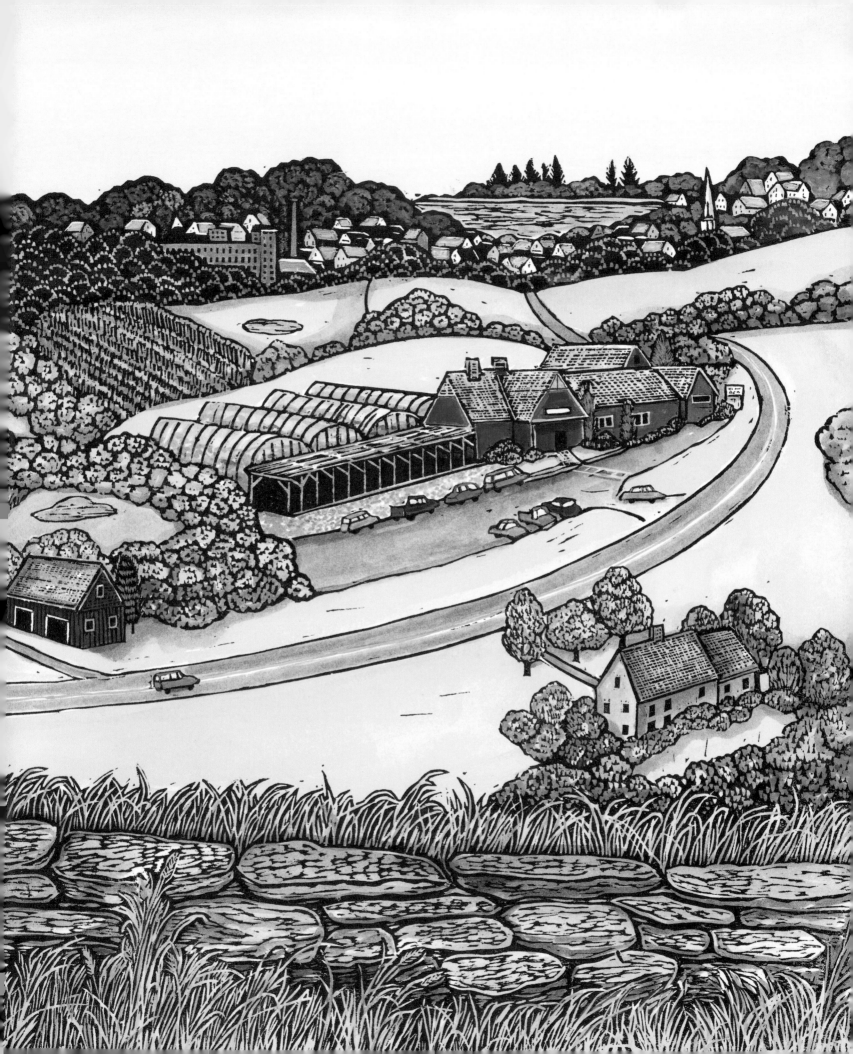

The Tuttle family's devotion to the land is unflagging. What was once a tiny farm stand is now over 9,000 square feet with an adjacent nursery. More than 1,000 customers shop at the Red Barn every day. The Tuttle farm is the oldest continuing family farm in America.